I Was Tired Today

I Was Tired Today

by

Marsha Brown Woodard

I Was Tired Today
©2011 by Marsha Brown Woodard

Publisher: brown bridges press
ISBN-13: 9781889819358

Dedication

This book is dedicated:

...With thanksgiving to God, who called me into this ministry and who has surrounded me at every stage of the journey with a great host of men and women. They have served as my midwives, mentors, colleagues, sistah-friends and brother-friends, biological and spiritual families, congregational members and students who each in their own way have been a vital part of me being able to live out this call.

...With appreciation for the many opportunities that others have extended to me to include my sermons, articles, and curriculum in their books. And to those who have encouraged me to write and who have prayed for the day when a book would be birthed.

...With hope that my journey, and the journey of women in my ministerial generation, will only be a shadow of the wonderful things that God will do through clergywomen in the current ministerial generation and the generations yet to come.

...With love to the women of the Priscilla Institute; God has used and continues to use you individually and collectively to bless my life and ministry.

Table of Contents

Dedication iii
Table of Contents v
The Journey Begins 1
I Was Tired Today 5
    I Was Tired Today 7
    Color Still Matters 11
    I Had Already Grieved 13
    Beyond Cost 15
    Sometimes 17
Uniquely Designed, Powerfully Called 21
    Sisters Made In the Image of God 23
    Unique Not Different 25
    Standing 29
    We Call Forth 33
    Memories 37
    Wonder of Wonders (WOW) 39
Seasons Will Change 43
    My Now and My When 45
    And Afterward 49
    Begin Again 53
    Ready Now 57
    Overflow 61
Pull It Forward 65
    Where is the New Kitchen? 67
    It Won't Matter 71
    The Thread 75
    God is Sending Power from on High 79
    Thank You 81
    References 83
About the Author 85

The Journey Begins

The book that you are now holding is a collection of reflections that grow out of my journey of being an African American woman, who is also clergy and who has been on the journey for awhile. Now having served over 30 years as an ordained minister I can attest to times of great joy as well as times of great pain. But even so, if God were to give me a choice of living life over again, I would choose to live at this time and be who I have become and am becoming: a preacher-pastor-professor-midwife who loves God and God's people.

Sometimes it was the gentle guidance of a midwife. Sometimes it was the helpful advice of a mentor. While at other times it was sitting at table with friends and in the conversations answers came. God has been a very real presence through it all and used it all to grow me.

I invite you to share the journey as you read this book by making it your own.

This is a talk back book so mark it up, add your thoughts, journal, and let it be the seed through which God births something in you.

I pray that this book will be a midwife, mentor, or friend at this time on your journey. I hope that it will become your book and that you will see it as a springboard to the thoughts that lie within you. Throughout the book there will opportunities for you to stop and think about what you have read. I call them places to Brood and Ponder, to allow the Holy Spirit to hover over your spirit and to speak to the deep and maybe not so deep places in you.

Blessings as you journey!

BROOD AND PONDER

Throughout the book BROOD AND PONDER pages are included. These are places to pause, slow down and reflect on what you have been reading.

- Allow the printed questions to begin, but not limit, your reflections.
- You may find it helpful to keep a journal close by where you can record your thoughts.
- If writing feels a bit too much, speak your thoughts into a digital recorder.

Who knows? God might be birthing a book in you, and your brooding will be the womb in which your thoughts grow.

I Was Tired Today

"*Because my skin is brown ...no matter the shade ... light, fair, dark, deep and comely, coco, honey caramel ... Brown skin makes others take notice ... Brown skin - skin with a permanent tan ... it doesn't fade ... it does not go away ... beautiful brown skin But because my skin is brown...life is not always easy*"

Marsha Brown Woodard

5

I Was Tired Today

I was tired today because I sat in another meeting and once again it was said that, "all of the administrative assistants were female and all the pastors were male."

I was tired today, because it was another day and another meeting where another male said something that women have been saying for years about race and now because a male said it - it was heard like a brand new revelation ...

I was tired today – because it was another time and another meeting where indeed it just seemed that being female and clergy is always needing to be the one to call or question the sexism, racism, whatever ism and always feeling like an interloper at the table. I was tired today ...

I was tired today of a struggle that never seems to end, of feeling the weight of being Black
      and female
         and clergy.

I was tired today and wondering why do I keep doing this, this cycle that never seems to end.

Yes, I was tired, real tired today!

But then I remembered, that there had been other women, other clergywomen, other women of color who didn't even get to sit at the table; who did not get invited to the meeting, who were so ignored that they weren't even able to call somebody's craziness into question

I was tired ... until I remembered that at the point when this had been new for me, at the point when I believed I could make a difference, at the point when I was learning how committees work and had not yet learned the subtleness of liberal racism and sexism, I remember even then there had been some clergywoman, some person of color who had been working for years trying to change the attitudes of others and I imagine they had a whole lot of days when they had been tired but they had not given up the struggle.

I was tired today until I remembered that I stand on the shoulders of my sisters and yes even some brothers who for centuries have been working that this might be a place, a world in which we're all able to live. I was tired until I remembered the women who have sacrificed for visions that they never saw fulfilled and for opportunities they never experienced.

I was tired today but then I remembered and was reminded that God is just calling me to join in the struggle; God is just calling me to be faithful in the season that is mine God is just calling me to continue the work that has already been started

I was tired and then I remembered that God is not calling me to be the completer of the work, God is not calling me to finish the work, God is just calling me to be as faithful in my day as so many others have been in theirs

So I am not tired anymore I've been renewed as I remember: That God yet calls me God's daughter, That it is yet God that called me into ministry That God yet has my face carved on the palm of his hand and That God is yet rejoicing over me

I was tired today ... but then I remembered!!

BROOD AND PONDER

> When have you been tired on your journey?

> Is tired the same for you as weary?

> Who have been the forerunners on your journey?

> If your could have a conversation with someone who paved the way for you that you never met, who would it be and what would you say

Color Still Matters

By the way, color still matters
No matter how much Euro-Americans protest
to the contrary- in these United States, skin
color still matters.

The people on the birthday cards, anniversary
cards, graduation cards are still white and so if
color didn't matter they could make cards with
brown people on them.
But I guess Euro-American people won't buy a
card with a brown person
And people of color have learned not to expect
to find themselves on the cards...
Color still matters

Color still matters because for the most part
only the obituaries and the weddings of Euro
American make the papers
It still matters because the people making to
many decisions are Euro-American
Color simply still matters

And while we can not deny that progress has
been made we do well to not forget that Euro
Americans still expect to be in charge and
Color simply still matters

11

BROOD AND PONDER

∂° Think back over the last week to places or situations in which you were aware of the subtle - and not so subtle - impact of skin color

∂° Over the next few days, pay attention to advertisements / commercials. When do you see People of Color? When do you see Euro-Americans? Do you notice any patterns?

∂° What do you think the world look like if skin color did not matter?

I Had Already Grieved

I had already grieved.
They were not physically dead but I had
grieved relationships that could not grow
grieved their unwillingness to move from
unhealth to health

I had grieved the pain
    the hurt
            the disappointments
                the betrayal of my trust
 the tears have already been shed

Yes, I had already grieved because the
relationship was already dead

It was when I discovered I was not valued for
me and that I was only welcomed if I played
by their rules. It was when I decided to no
longer play the games and that truth was
important. When I decided that my feelings did
matter, and I was willing to admit that the way
I was being treated really did hurt.

That is when the grieving occurred that's when
the tears were shed
Don't ask me to grieve now, for I've already
grieved.

BROOD AND PONDER

∾ Grief is a process and a journey unique to each person. Think of times of loss in your life and how you have grieved.

∾ When relationships end with physical death grief is expected but when they end for other reasons sometimes it is hard to give ourselves permission to grieve. Reflect on your journey looking for any suppressed grief and if there is take time to begin the grieving process.

Beyond Cost

There are some things that money cannot buy
        Some things that you cannot ask for
                Some things that you cannot place on
lay-away, or lease, or borrow

 There are some things that money cannot buy

There are some things that can only be given
        Things that once given are better than a
million, billion, trillion dollars
        Things that remind you that the Spirit of
God is always at work
        Things that are a precious gift

Today I received such a gift
        Unexpected
            Caught me by surprise
                A gift to treasure for a lifetime

"I'm sorry ... it was a bad decision ...
        ...I made it too quickly ... I'm sorry"

To some those may just be words, but for me,
they were a gift more valuable than words can
express, priceless and always to be valued

 There are some things that money just
cannot buy

BROOD AND PONDER

❧ When have you received a gift from another person that was valuable beyond cost?

❧ What was a gift that you have given someone else that they might say was valuable beyond cost?

Sometimes

Sometimes the blessing comes long before the
sermon begins ... .

Sometimes it isn't a paragraph or even a whole
sentence, that becomes a healing balm,

Sometimes it is not the length of what is said
and it may not even have been the speakers'
intent for those words to make a particular
impact

Yet sometimes God will take words and
transform them as they travel across the
airwaves and they will land on your ears with a
power that impacts your spirit and leaves you
speechless

Sometimes you come to the service simply to
worship and praise God ... you come to
simply gather with the Saints and glorify God.

You expect to meet God but there is no special
request, no identified need, just the blessing
that comes from worshipping God

And Sometimes God will surprise you

And send healing when you didn't know you
needed to be healed ... move at a place in the
service where you did not expect it.

Sometimes it is not in the music,
      the prayer
          the sermon
             or even the fellowship

Sometimes, in a second, a place
      deep within you is healed and revived

Tonight was such a time for me, just a few
words, part of a sentence, in the midst of a
statement of purpose ... but I was blessed
beyond measure by them and I began to
praise and thank God for allowing me to
experience this moment in time because

Sometimes the blessing comes in an
unexpected place

BROOD AND PONDER

- ❧ When have you been surprised by God in the midst of worship?

- ❧ Sometimes our pain becomes numb, we grow accustom to it and are no longer praying for healing, yet God still has the power to heal and will heal without our asking. Think of times and situations when you have experienced the healing power of God

Uniquely Designed, Powerfully Called

"I stood in the total authenticity of my being - Black, Preacher, Baptist, Woman . For the same God who made me a preacher made me a woman. And I am convinced that God was not confused on either count"

Praitha Hall

"To Live As if the Truth is True"

Trinette McRay

Sisters Made In the Image of God

Not in our own image
Or the image of some movie star
Not in the image of one another
Nor the image of our parents, friends and kin
We are sisters made in the image of God,
Yes, the image of God

You see we were made, created, uniquely
designed by God
We're a one of a kind ... an original design ...
no one else like us
Because we are, Sisters, who are made in the
Image of God

When we look in the mirror we see the
reflection of God
When we look at one another we see the
reflection of God
Even though we are short and tall,
Various shades of brown
Young and not so young
We are yet precious, for we are made in the
image of God

We are sisters, women of color, sisters in the
body of Christ, sisters made in the image of
God

23

Brood and Ponder

- Stand in front of a mirror and say, "I am made in the image of God!" at least 5 times.

Unique Not Different

Different ... not the same as ... other than
... not like ...
I've decided, yes, I've made up my mind ...
I'm throwing the word different yes Dif-fer-ent
out of my vocabulary ...
yes it is gone, no longer in my personal
dictionary.
I'm tired of measuring up to standards that
someone else created in their heads
I'm tired and I don't think I want to play the
game any longer ...
So no more Different - because I thought of a
fresh idea ...
or I wore something that concerned somebody
or my race or my gender and even my age
stood out before I even opened my mouth ...
so while you may think I'm different and
maybe even that is your code to say you
believe I'm an outsider, a part of your out
group, that I don't belong and I'm not welcome
at your party ...
It's ok ... because I woke up this morning
and I realized I'm not different I'm just unique
and I've decided I'm not playing the game any
longer,
I'm going to unlearn the messages you have
been sending making me feel that something
was wrong with me
No - different ... it's not in my vocabulary any
more. I've got a new word ... a word that

makes me feel whole, a word that makes me
smile ... Unique, yes but not different
I am simply unique
You see I am a one of a kind creation
I'm a designer original
oh yes I was uniquely shaped and formed in
my mother's womb
I've been created for purposes uniquely
designed for me.
I'm headed to my own destiny and to places
that only I can go
There is only one of me, no copies here, no
duplication,
the pattern was thrown away,
See I'm not different I'm unique a designer
original ... a one of a kind creation
Since the foundation of the world God has
been waiting for just this time to send me to
earth, I didn't come a moment too soon and I
am not a second too late. It has all been
designed with me in mind ... and since God
thinks I am special and precious and rejoices
over me with singing, I've decided that I am
going to learn to trust God's messages because
I feel better being unique than I ever felt being
different.

But hey! Let me tell you a secret: you are
unique too, you're a one of kind creation, a
designer original, your pattern has been
destroyed ... no one else will ever be just like
you
You are not just one in a million but you are
one in a zillion billion trillion quadrillion ...

one in the universe oh my sister and yes my
brother
you are unique, a designer original ... a one of
a kind creation ... Uniquely designed to make
a unique impact in the kingdom

So since I am unique and you are unique let's
rejoice and give a crazy kind of praise, that
God is a God who never gets tired of creating
designer originals, one of a kind creation ...
women and men just like us who are fearfully
and wonderfully made ... unique but never
different. We are designer originals ... One of
a kind creation

BROOD AND PONDER

❧ List at least 5 unique gifts / talents you have.

❧ Describe at least 5 ways God is using you to impact the kingdom.

❧ Think about five friends. For each one of them write down what their 5 unique gifts or talents are and 5 ways each of them is impacting the Kingdom.

Standing

Standing here ... standing here ... in this place ... at this juncture ... in this season ... on this day ... in this month ... .I'm standing here

See!! Look!! See, I am standing here ... it is me ... and yet I am not standing here alone

Look! ... Can't you see them? They are here ...

> My sister friends

> > My Mother in the faith friends ...

> > > My 'auntie in the gospel' friends

> > > My friends of other friends,

> > > No, I'm not standing alone

Can't you see I am standing here with the women from yesterday and yesteryear,

the women who heard a call and when they responded everyone said no it cannot be ...

I'm standing with the women who responded but the way was so hard they didn't get very far ... I'm standing with the women who saw the vision afar but did not see it fulfilled ...

I'm standing here ... standing here ... in this place ... at this juncture ... in this season ... on this day ... in this month ... .I'm standing here

And I am surrounded - surrounded - surrounded by a great cloud of witnesses

The witnesses who were willing to stand on the promises of God

Women willing to stand when the doors were slammed in their face

Women willing to stand and believe when the dream was delayed, denied, deferred

Women willing to stand when there was no yet not a highway, a lane, a road, a path

Women willing to stand when the vision felt more like a nightmare than a dream

Women willing to stand in the midst of the abuses and pain

Women who kept standing on the promises of God

So yes I am standing here but I am standing on holy ground yes I know that there are angels all around

I can see Jesus, now for I am standing in this place and this is holy ground

Surrounded by this cloud of witnesses I am ready to pick up my weary feet, I am ready to have my soul renewed, I am ready to run the race that is set before me ... Because if I am surrounded then the cloud is cheering me on they are wishing me well they have my back and

And so God do a new thing in me ... God use me for your glory, God endow me with new power ...

Because I am standing ready to do your will

    Standing ready to blaze my own path

        Standing ready to carry the dream
a little further

            Standing ready to be the
answer to someone's prayer

                Standing ready to be
the woman you have called
me to be

Yes, I am Standing here ... standing here ... in
this place ... at this juncture ... in this season
... on this day ... in this month ...

    and I am grateful that I am never
standing alone but that I am always
surrounded

BROOD AND PONDER

ঙ What God given promises are you standing
   on waiting for their fulfillment?

ঙ Who are the people on your cloud of
   witnesses, cheering you on?

ঙ Have there been times when you have
   forgotten that you are surrounded? If so,
   what did that feel like; and what led you to
   remember the cloud of witnesses?

We Call Forth

We call forth the vision and the dream
We call forth the hope that lies deep within
We call forth all that God would do in you
My sisters of a new generation

We call forth the courage to walk in faith
We call forth belief that God will do all that God
has promised
We call forth the courage to walk in new ways
We call forth the willingness to live in seasons
of overflow
We call forth the ability that is within

We, your sisters in ministry who started in a
day different than your own,
Call forth in you the possibilities that we didn't
dare to dream
And that sometimes we didn't know to dream
We call forth the courage to walk in places that
we could not walk

We call forth freedom from the bondages that
enslaved us
We call forth freedom from the bondages that
would now enslave you

We call forth pastors of small congregations
and pastors of medium sized congregations
and pastors of mega congregations
We call forth the willingness to create new
forms of ministry

We call forth the secret dreams and the
unshared visions

We call forth the prayers that you have prayed
We call for strength to wait for the answers
that only God can send
We call forth the willingness and the ability to
trust the process
We call forth joy even in the midst of sorrow
We call forth dancing in the midst of defeat
and praise in the midst of pain

O my sisters, O women of God, O generation
too numerous to count
O Women of God, You who will be preachers
You who will be chaplains , associates,
ministers of outreach, pastors, professors,
youth ministers, creators and founders of
ministries We call you forth

We call you forth: with the power within us
We call you forth: from the tears we have shed
We call you forth: knowing that your road will
not always be easy
We call you forth: because we know the same
God who has led and kept us will lead and
keep you
We call you forth: Go now and serve!

BROOD AND PONDER

❧ What will it look like for women to start their ministerial journey from a place different than previous generations?

❧ For the generation of clergywomen who start their career from a place where they are respected and accepted, what difference might it make in their own understanding of their call to ministry?

❧ What will this new generation need to know from the past; and what might be the challenges they will face?

❧ If you are a member of the "new" generation what do you believe has been called forth by your predecessors? And what do you think will need to be called forth in the ministerial generation that follows you?

Memories

Written for: Nina Baker, Cheryl Brame, Sandra Byrd, Cherly Vaughn Curry, Michelle Ford Johnson, Janice Roberts, Yvonne Shaw, Gail Taylor, Margaret Trice, Denise Twyman, and Denise White members of the first Priscilla Institute Cohort as they completed their Associate Degree

The memories tumble out ... the memories
they just tumble out ... I look at you,
     I think of you and the memories simply
tumble out ...
The first day I met you is so different from
today -- So much space between then and now
... Oh yes, the memories tumble out

There is joy and sorrow
     Excitement and despair
          Days of longing and nights of tears
     Memories, Memories, Memories ...
     that tumble tumble, tumble ... out

And yet a single thread connects with every
memory
     A consistent thread that has always been
there
     Sometimes seen and sometimes outside
     of view

God has always been there
     With every memory that tumbles out I
see God's hand in your lives, in this program,
in my life and in the lives of others ... Flooding
me with Memories that cannot be contained

And so I thank God for each of you I bless
God's name for your journey
You have done well individually and
collectively.
　　　You have walked on uncharted waters
　　　Held on when it would have been easy to
give up. Through you God has turned dreams
and visions into realty.

I thank God for your journey; I thank God for
the women of God that you are. I thank God
for the memories that tumble,
　　　tumble,
　　　　　tumble out,
　　　　　　like a flood!!

Wonder of Wonders (WOW)

WOW
  Wonder of Wonders
    This day has arrived!!
You saw it ... we saw it
      Dimly ... ... Dimly
Yet course by course it has grown brighter
    And Now
WOW ... ... Wonder of Wonders
      This day has arrived!!!
The impossible has become possible
    The unseen is now seen
      Great has been God's
    faithfulness ... WOW ---
    Wonder of Wonders This day has arrived
God has been faithful through the days and the weeks
    Faithful through every course and every assignment
    Faithful through every trial and disappointment
    Faithful through every joy an achievement
    Faithful from the beginning
    Faithful still at the end
Wonder of wonders
This day has arrived!!!!
    The program is completed
      The course work is done
      Graduation is on the horizon

Wow ... Wonder of Wonders - this day has arrived
Praise God!
Praise God!!!

Praise God!!!!

BROOD AND PONDER

❧ When have you been happy for another's success?

❧ Have there been times when you achieved a goal that you thought at the beginning was impossible to accomplish?

❧ Reflect on your journey and the places where God has been faithful to you beyond measure.

Seasons Will Change

"As Jesus was dying they pierced him in the side and out came blood mingled with water. He was birthing new life even as he was dying. Women as they are giving birth have blood mixed with water as they die to parts of themselves even as they are giving birth to a new life"

DeAndra M. Richardson

My Now and My When

What is the work I need to do ___NOW___ so that it will be different___WHEN___
What is the work you need to do **NOW** so that it will be different **WHEN**

My **NOW** is preparing me for my **WHEN** and Your **NOW** is preparing you for your **WHEN**

This is not the work of 'I think I am better or I think someone is less than effective than they should be' ... No this is the work of *being faithful* to what *God is birthing* in me

What kind of pastor is God calling you to be ... What kind of Director of an Agency ... What kind of church school teacher ... choir director ... youth leader?

There is a work in your **NOW** that is preparing you for your **WHEN**

My **WHEN** work might look different from my **NOW** and others might not see a direct connection but there is something in my **NOW** that is getting me ready for a **WHEN** I cannot see ... maybe cannot even imagine

What do I understand about leadership? How will I work with others? What do I value?

These are the questions you have to ask now before the when occurs ... in order for my when to not just replicate others now

Now is the place to struggle with the questions Now is the place to look at options Now is the time to read books and look at many models

Now is the time to get in touch with your own demands and your own needs

Now is the place to work on you

For when **WHEN** happens there won't be time to think about a new model ... .When **WHEN** happens if you don't already have a new model ... a different understanding ... if you haven't already tried something new

When **WHEN** occurs you will simply repeat whatever has been done in the past ... you will do whatever has always been done ... you will not make changes ... simply because in your **NOW** you failed to do the work that would allow your **WHEN** to be different

Your NOW is preparing YOU for your WHEN

BROOD AND PONDER

᪥ What is God calling you to today that is different from the call of the past?

᪥ What did you use to do that you really cannot do anymore?

᪥ Who are you preventing from growing because you won't give it up, move over, or give them some space to be who God is calling them to become?

And Afterward

After you have struggled and failed
After the hurt and the pain
After the sorrow and shame

      God will pour
      God will pour
      God will pour (softer)

After the wilderness
After the exile
After the journey that never seemed to end

      God will pour
          God   will   pour
      God will pour

After disappointment
After betrayal
After heartbreak

      God will pour
          God will pour !!!!!!
    GOD   WILL   POUR !!!!!

Pour joy for sorrow
      Pour hope for despair
            Pour peace for turmoil

joy for sorrow....hope for despair... peace for
turmoil

After it all ... our God pours

Pours newness and a new way
Pours new strength and vision
Pours a new season

And after it all

"God will pour out his spirit on all flesh

Sons and daughters will prophesy
Daughters and Sons will prophesy

The Young will dream and the old will have
visions"

And It shall be
It shall be
It shall be

(fade out voice)
And Afterwards ... ..
God will
Pour....

BROOD AND PONDER

- The door was closed but that does not mean the door is still closed: pray for the space to believe that your "now" can be different than your "was."

- The "Afterward" season means there has been a change. What changes do you need to make for the new season?

Begin Again

Lord help me to begin again
             Start out ... Fresh
                    Have a Clean Slate
                           I want Lord, to begin
                    again ...

Lord I need to let the past be the past -
             Release the shoulda' woulda'
coulda's
                    Lord send me a clean page ...
                           And let me begin again.

You forget Lord ... ...
             You cast my sins in your sea of
forgetfulness;
                    But I can't forget, I rehearse them
             over and over again;
                           I bear the guilt and I feel the
                    shame,
                           I wear the
                           disappointment and then
                           bear more pain!

Please God, help me to begin again.
             To let the old be gone and to allow the
new to appear -
                    Again and again tell me:
                           I am your begotten child
                           You Tell me
                                  I am fearfully and
                    wonderfully made

53

Lord, please help me to
Believe again ...
Dream again ... ...
Trust again ... ...
Even hope again

Please speak to my heart, Lord, and speak to
my soul
Empower my spirit Lord;
teach me to soar!
Because I just want Lord to begin
again-
To be better than I was and
on my way to what I will be ...

Lord if you just do it
I know that this can be, will be, shall be
a new year –
a great year - a year to begin
again

Lord if you just do it ...
Just strengthen me ... just lead me ...
Just empower me ... just guide me
... just love me ...
... Just be my God

Then Lord I will be able to BEGIN AGAIN

BROOD AND PONDER

Ș Since it's been long enough to have fear-disappointment-despair-hurt-pain-anger-low self esteem ... Long enough to hold pity parties, to think you can't succeed or the situation won't change, what do you need to give up so that you can start fresh?

Ș To speak life is to state those things that will bring life in its fullness. Speaking life is not just smooth sounding words but speaking life is helping others to grow. In what ways are you being called to speak life to yourself? To your situation?

Ș How can you bless yourself and bless others as a way to have a fresh start and begin again?

Ready Now

I'm ready now- I'm ready from within—
I'm ready now; I'm ready from within,
Ready for whatever lies ahead,
ready for roads I do not know,
Ready for paths I have not trod and for
ways I cannot see.
I'm ready, I'm ready, I'm ready now, I'm
ready from within.

For something's been happening -- happening
deep inside of me--
It's been growing and pushing and pulling and
stretching me and now ...
I'm ready -- I'm ready from within

It's coming forth, it will change my life I will
never be the same
and I am ready, for I've been changed from
within
Ready because I've learned to depend not on
myself,
not even on my friends ...
and education was not enough,
nor anything else that I could see or
comprehend

I'm ready because I've learned to lean ... LEAN
... and to depend ...
RADICALLY DEPEND ON GOD ...

Ready because I know that nothing can
separate me from God's love
I know that if everything is gone and only God
is left that is enough.... enough, ENOUGH to
begin again

Ready because it was God who has been ... has
been ... preparing me—
It was God who has been getting me ready,

Since the beginning of time, God has had plans
for me, yes me,
Plans for this time and for this thing,
   this opportunity,
   for this season in my life--

I'm ready because I've been made ready, yes,
I'm ready from within

And so I can say Yes to his way and Yes to his
will
  I can have an Esther if I perish I perish YES
  An Abraham leave my homeland and go to
a place I have never been YES
  A Shiprah and Puah refuse to follow the
king's edict YES
  A Jochebed hid my baby YES
  A Miriam and David dance before the Lord
YES
  A Daughters of Zelophehad had claim our
inheritance YES
  A Job if he slay me yet will I serve him YES
  A Jeremiah fire in my bones YES

A Mary let it be unto me according to your will, YES

And even if it means a cross YES

I'm ready because I've been made ready,
       yes, I'm ready from within

BROOD AND PONDER

- Claim the truth and power inside of yourself.

- Along with your "big girl" coat (fur, leather or suede), your "big girl" shoes (be they heels or boots), and your "big girl" position, you need "Big Girl" Faith in order to go out and transform the world. How is God stretching you and growing your faith so that you will be able to pull up your pantyhose, step into your heels, and confidently say, "Yes I'm ready to go out and transform the world!"?

Overflow

Overflow, overflow, this is the year of God's
overflow
An outpouring of love, sent from above- this is
the year of God's overflow
Every promise of God now is yes and amen –
What God said is now done, the battle now
won,
Overflow ... Overflow ... Yes, this is the year
of God's overflow!!!

What you thought would not be, God is letting
you see,
    - it was delayed not denied and it has
come to be ...
        Beyond all your dreams and much
    more than you expected,
            - though others said no
God has said yes.
            Delayed for a
season but now it is here,

Overflow this is the year of God's overflow

So stretch out and look up restoration is now,
Throw up the windows and look all around,
Yes open the doors for blessings are coming
down ...
Sent straight from God's throne,
The flow is unceasing, cannot be contained,
For this is the season of God's overflow

To the east or the west, to the north or the south,
>To the right or the left, to the front or the back
>>You still are surrounded, the blessings still flowing.
>>>God's joyous surprises are now all around you
>>>>Your tears now are laughter
>>>>Your sorrow now joy,
>>>>>Burst forth into singing
>>>>>For this is overflow

Look all around you the season has changed,
No longer in exile you have been reclaimed.
All that was taken has now been restored,
No longer forsaken you have been named,
God calls you his child and says,
>"Look up and see the showers of blessings I'm sending, and receive.
>For I am the giver of every good gift, and now in this season I want you to learn that I am the God who will bountifully bless."

So walk now in victory, and do not delay, the way has been made.
The battles are over, the season has changed.
The future is glorious your best yet to be!!
Now lift high your voice, praise God and rejoice,
For this is the season of blessings beyond measure.
It's Overflow ... Overflow
This is the year of God's overflow

BROOD AND PONDER

   What changes in attitude will you need to make from being in a season of scarcity to now being in a season of overflow?

   In times of scarcity sometimes there is a tendency to hoard; in seasons of abundance there is often more of a willingness to freely share. What gifts / talents have you hoarded in the past that you can now freely share?

Pull It Forward

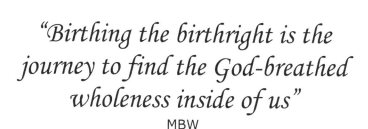

"Birthing the birthright is the journey to find the God-breathed wholeness inside of us"

MBW

Where is the New Kitchen?

Where is the new kitchen?
For the generation that doesn't cook,
no longer is cleaning greens nor pickin' chitlins'
clean ...

When we stop at the bar- be -que place or the
soul food diner to pick up the potato salad
And we have finally found the bakery that
makes yeast rolls - while not as good as
Aunt Susie Mae ... or Mother Sister Jones at
the church ... but they will do ...
          for we are the generation that doesn't
get up early in the morning,
               at least not to roll dough and let yeast
               rise

Where is the kitchen table????...
          the place for the women to gather?
in this generation where we aren't gathering
around the stove with one head being pressed
while another head is being washed, and the
baby girl is getting her hair braided as she sits
between her momma's knees

Where do the women gather?

In this generation when we live hundreds and
thousands of miles away from the sisters
we grew up with and we work in places where
we are the 'only' one,

Just where is it pray tell that the women gather?

Where do the women gather , when our education has us in the position to be the boss and the only other sister in the place is mopping the floor ... where do we gather to share the stories and laugh the secret laughter and bear the joys and the pain ... to have a common experience?

Where did you say was the place / the gathering place / the place where the stories are shared, the place where we gain the courage to exist and to thrive and to live?

Where do the women gather when the church kitchen has a signed posted on the door, *Kitchen Closed?*

When the dinners are no longer cooked, catered maybe but not cooked, on the premises, where do the women gather? Who shares the stories, who remembers the journey, who has the dream for the next generation?

Where do the women gather?

What do we do when the generation that made the rolls and brought the sterling silver and had the name of the church monogrammed on it, and cleaned the greens and fought to have the best cake and stayed up nights making sweet potato pie ... What do we do when we their daughters and granddaughters are the generation of microwave and paper plates, disposable and frozen food, pay the caterer, make it simple but please don't ask me to cook...where do the women gather?

Where will the stories be shared? Where will the friendships be developed? Where are the problems being resolved in the midst of the work? Where is the anger abated as we share in the journey? Where do the sisters gather and share the heartache and share the great joy? Where do we hold one another accountable, and hold one another through the storm and the pain, where do we laugh and where do we learn to be strong and resilient Black women?

Now that the kitchen is closed ... and the sign is on the door...where -- can you tell me where ... ARE THE WOMEN ARE GATHERING?

BROOD AND PONDER

~ What images of the kitchen do you have?

~ What are / were the kitchens in your past?

~ Where are your kitchens now?

~ Who "sits" at your table?

It Won't Matter

They won't know that you came to the funeral
... won't appreciate that you pressed your way
even made some sacrifices to get there.

No they won't care that you missed the
appointment – changed your work schedule
shifted things around, so you could be there
They simply won't know

They won't hear the things you say – how
much you valued their friendship – how
precious they were to you – they won't hear
the compliments ... They won't see your tears
-- or hear the laughter as you reminisce

It just won't matter – the time for giving will
be over ... The funeral is a little too late!!

While I'm not sure who made the decision and
who sent out the decree that the funeral was
the place to show up, the time to make the
sacrifice ... that the funeral was important
enough to miss the meeting, change the
schedule, go even if you are tired ... I am not
sure who decided the funeral and not the
worship service, the graduation, the lunch
invitation, or any number of other important
occasions...

But I am sure that the funeral is really too late
because the deceased will not even know that

you cared enough to come. They will not hear any of the wonderful things that are said, nor smell the flowers.

So new decree new decision new thought ... why not press your way today to support a friend ... switch a meeting around this week and change that appointment today. Because now your friend will know, now they will be aware that you care. Now it will matter... and if you decide to wait, remember the funeral will just be too late.

BROOD AND PONDER

☙ Plan an "I Appreciate and Value You" week. During this week you will let at least one person a day know how much they are appreciated by doing acts of kindness. Send a thinking of you card; take them out for coffee or lunch; show up for a presentation they are making, etc. You are letting them know that they are important to you while they are still able to experience your love, appreciation or respect for them.

☙ Examine your calendar and treat some invitations or appointments with the same urgency you would give to a funeral of a close friend or relative. Know, by doing this, the person you are meeting or spending time with, will be able to actually see and feel that you care.

The Thread

Maybe threads … .maybe more than one …
but the thread has always been pulled forward
… forward
Forward to the future not to the past … it has
always been pulled … pulled … pulled forward
It goes back, not the thread but the process
… back not sure how
Far … maybe all the way back to the
beginning of time
     But the thread … the threads … were
never lost … they have never been lost
Not from the ships bringing Africans to
become slaves … not from the extinction of
tribal people … not during apartheid in South
Africa … no matter the challenge … how great
the injustice … there has always been
someone pulling the thread forward … forward
to the future
     Threads not broken no matter how
fragile … or tangled
There has been someone … some ones …
individuals … groups … .many ones … single
ones … always someone to pull … .t o p u l l
t o   P U L L

P U L L
     Pull   PULL   the
    thread forward
Forward to the next generation …
forward so the story is not lost …
Pull the thread … for … ward

Our sisters have done it ... we must learn their names ... ... their stories must become our story ... then we will call their names and grab the thread and pull ... pull. Pull it forward. I see them the women with doors being shut in their face ... .I hear them the sisters crying out and no one seems to hear ... They are looking and wondering will we take the thread ...
We paved the way ... we dreamed the dream ... ... we knew this day would come ... ... let our living not be in vain ... ... Can't you hear them ... don't you see them ... holding the thread ... ... wondering will we grab the end ... ... will we have the courage for this age and this season ... ... Will we walk the uncharted road ... ...

Thread Pullers the world needs thread pullers ... ... and since we are here because of the faith of our sisters we ought to Grab a thread and Let God's will be done in us.
Grab the thread... and pull it forward as we continue the kingdom work already begun
Pull the thread ... ... .forward

It's waiting for you!!! The thread is waiting for you to reach out ... ...
To grab on ... to carry it
Forward!!!

FORWARD!!! ...

FORWARD!!!!!

Pull it because there is work to be done and the 6th generation of clergywomen are depending on us!!!!

(The Thread was originally written August 1, 2009 as a Reflection on a Conversation with Dr. Donna Jones, about Dr. Vincent Harding. This version was written June 2011 for the Daughters of Thunder Conference for Clergywomen of Color.)

BROOD AND PONDER

God is the master weaver. God takes the hurt and disappointment, the joy and excitement and weaves them all together. God takes every side of the issue: the things we cannot resolve and the things we can and weaves them together.

- How is God taking your life situations and weaving them into a different present and future?

- What threads are you pulling forward into God's future?

God is Sending Power from on High

God is sending power from on high
To shape and to mold us,
Strengthen and empower us
To do his will, to do his will

We will be shepherds after God's heart
We will be shepherds after God's heart
To serve one another,
To teach, preach, and yes to lead
God's people here
God's people here God's people here

This will be a new year for us
This will be a new year for us
Our strength will be renewed
Our vision will be clearer
It will come to pass, come to pass

God will do a new thing in us
God will do a new thing in us
Much more than we've asked for and
More than we've prayed for
God will do much more, God will do more

(can also be sung to the tune "I Will Do a New Thing")

BROOD AND PONDER

To be ready for the new thing that God is doing
you may need to pray for the:
>Power to believe like Mary the Mother of Jesus
>Power to wait and trust God like Anna
>Power to act like the Midwives

- What is God birthing in you and how are you responding to the pregnancy?

- Write a prayer that will help you be ready to recognize, accept and deliver on the new thing that God is doing through you.

Thank You

Today I stop to say, Thank You to all the people I didn't know to thank:

The people who have spoken a kind word in my favor in the meetings that I didn't attend

The people who have mentored me from afar with their prayers

The people who have sat on boards and committees making decisions that have impacted my life I say thank you because there have been open doors and new opportunities that have blessed me because of the decisions that you made.

The behind the scenes folk who have contributed to my welfare without me ever knowing, today, I simply say thank you.

The people who spoke a word and placed my name before the committee and it led to an invitation to teach or to preach, thank you.

So today, I simply say thank you to the many people I didn't know to thank, and who I may never meet, please accept my gratitude for you have made a great difference in my journey and I have been bountifully blessed.

BROOD AND PONDER

~ Pray a prayer of thanksgiving for the help that you have received from unknown sources.

~ Ask God to show you situations where you have been blessed so you can go back and give thanks to someone for helping you.

~ Have there been times or situations that initially did not seem to be good that God has now worked for good, and has used to be a blessing to your life or ministry?

References

Section Page Quotes

I Was Tired Today

Marsha Brown Woodard, "Brown Skin" from *Birthing the Birthright: Midwife Leadership Style With African American Clergywomen*, page 29.

Uniquely Designed, Powerfully Called

Rev. Dr. Prathia Hall, quoted in *Birthing the Birthright: Midwife Leadership Style With African American Clergywomen*, by Marsha Brown Woodard, page 7. Marsha Brown Woodard

Rev. Dr. Trinette McCray, from sermon delivered 2010 Together in the Lord Conference, Orlando Florida. (audio CD)

Seasons Will Change

Mrs. DeAndra M. Richardson, from a conversation with the author. (10/26/2006)

Pull It Forward

Marsha Brown Woodard

About the Author
Marsha Brown Woodard

Rev. Dr. Marsha Brown Woodard is a pastor, preacher, midwife educator, friend, sister and colleague who resides in the suburbs of Philadelphia.

Ordained in 1980, during her early years of ministry as an American Baptist clergywoman she and her friends either knew (or knew someone who did know) all of the African American clergywomen in that denomination. It was equally true, as well, that there were not large numbers of clergywomen in other denominations.

She is excited that the number of African American clergywomen within all denominations is now too vast to be counted, that congregations more readily are calling women to serve, and that there are so many opportunities for ministry that did not exist at the beginning of her journey.

Dr. Woodard currently serves as Lecturer in Christian Ministry and as an Academic Advisor at the Palmer Theological Seminary in Wynnewood, Pa. She has served as pastor or a member of the pastoral staff for congregations in both Pennsylvania and Missouri. She maintains ministerial standing with the American Baptist Churches USA, National Baptist Churches, Inc and the Christian Church (Disciples of Christ).

18690400R00050

Made in the USA
Charleston, SC
16 April 2013